MERCY LEADER

Transforming People with Mercy

MERCY LEADER

Transforming People with Mercy

Dr. Jeffrey A. Radford

Dr. Jeff Radford

mercyspeaks@drjeffradford.com

https://www.drjeffradford.com

CONTENTS

ACKNOWLEDGMENTS

In 2007, God birthed the concept of merciful leadership into my heart to share with others. I personally know about mercy because I experience it from others but more importantly, God continues to extend mercy and grace into my life. I am forever grateful for His unconditional love.

I want to thank my wife, Debbie, for always being my support, best friend, and the "rock" of our family. I appreciate her for always being there to listen to my ideas, and my words will never be able to express the love and gratitude I have for her. To my daughter, Kaitlyn, thank you for making me believe I am your "Super Hero". I am proud of the young lady you have become. To my son, Blake, I am proud of you and grateful that God allowed me to be your dad. To all of my other family and friends, thank you for listening to my project ideas. There are many influencers in my life, and I am grateful that God has brought them into my journey!

PREFACE

From a young age, I have always had a passion to serve others. Not only is serving others my passion, I have learned it is my purpose. My journey through life has allowed me to deepen this purpose and actually define my leadership approach. While attending my doctoral program at Regent University, I was preparing for the final project. This was a challenging task because I wanted the topic to be perfect and cumulate my studies for the past three and a half years. As the search for the perfect topic continued, I had a defining moment. My mind reflected on past experiences with leaders, my studies of different leadership paradigms, and my own limited leadership career. God birthed the concept of merciful leadership into my soul, and from there, the words began to flow.

I want to introduce to you a leadership paradigm I believe will be very beneficial to you and your ability to transform yourself and other people. Several years after this defining moment a mercy leader has become clearer, and the characteristics continue to exhibit the transformation of others. We live in a troubled world, and I predict there will always be significant world incidents, organizational challenges, and life situations. Some type of problem will always be there. Some type of decision will always need to be made. There will be positive times in our lives and careers, and there will also be negative times. It's during these challenges and situations that strong leadership is required.

During these times, what are people searching for? They are seeking a leader who is consistent in his/her leadership approach.

They are also searching for a leader who values them and takes personal investment in their development and interests. Merciful leadership is not a weak approach to leadership. There is not time for weakness during these challenges. Merciful leadership is for those who are willing to be transformational in a challenging time. Merciful leadership is for those who are willing to have the courage to invest in others. Merciful leadership is for those who are willing to value others in a society that seems more centered around results than the people who achieve them. Are you ready to be a mercy leader? If so, I am honored to guide you through the characteristics that will assist you in transforming the lives of those you serve, and I am thankful you have taken the time to read this book.

—Dr. Jeff Radford

CHAPTER 1
JUDGMENT LEADERS

"Don't pick on people, jump on their failures, criticize their faults —unless, of course, you want the same treatment."

—Matthew 7:1, TM

"Usually our criticism of others is not because they have faults, but because their faults are different from ours."[1]

—Roger Eastman

You've seen them! Yes, you have seen judgmental leaders. They may have been the crusty bosses from the endless sitcoms we've all grown up watching on TV: stodgy old men passing down judgment from on high about how their employees were to look, behave, and perform. For many years, this stereotype has rung true. These judgmental leaders practice a dictator style of leadership. Their fingers pointed out and mostly likely said, "Do as I say." Unfortunately, they don't always expect the same of themselves as the demands they are giving to their team. It actually makes me wonder if they even have a team or are just programmed robots that have no value other than results, results, results...... They are dictators who rely on power to influence. Furthermore, this type of leadership creates a judgmental environment if the results are not achieved without looking for reasons. This judgement creates an environment of fear instead of respect. I know because I have been exposed to judgmental leaders and have found that their followers, including me, are more concerned with the judgement instead of developing a relationship with the leader. I have also found by personal experience that employees of these kinds of leaders often hide things from them so a situation will not be exacerbated by the leader's snap judgments.

As a child, I thought my parents were always barking orders and would be quick to condemn me when I messed up. I am sure my children have thought the same as they have grown up. Because of this imagined judgmental behavior, I was not very forthcoming with them when I did make mistakes. (Usually, they either found out later anyway or sometimes already knew because the guilt of my actions was written all over my face.) However, I look back on my childhood experience, and also see mercy. My parents only wanted the best for me and each moment of correction was a moment of investment in my development and future. However, judgmental leaders do not share the same values for those they lead.

Throughout my career and involvement with countless people, I have discovered a true fact. It is easier to be judgmental. That may take you by surprise, but when you evaluate leaders or maybe even yourself, the easy way is judging others. Why? It requires less work!

If we don't judge but actually take the time to consider all aspects of the situation, that action requires work and effort. Do you consider both sides of the story? The too-quick-to-judge mentality has caused me to make what I know now to be the wrong decision because I did not put forth the effort to consider both sides. I admit I have made the error of quickly judging employees because of mistakes. From these mistakes, I have learned important lessons. I have found myself wanting to discipline employees without looking at the reason for their mistake. This was mainly due to a lack of experience. However, it was unpleasant for the people, and it is not something that I am proud of. I have grown as a mercy leader, and wisdom and experience have taught me many lessons.

One lesson is to always ask the WHY. Get the facts before rushing to a decision. Why is the follower making the mistake? The issue may be the organization has failed them by not providing the proper training. Another issue is that people are unique and learn at a different pace. Judgmental leaders assume the follower will not improve and seek to move quickly to remove that person or better stated-remove the problem. Is this the best method for the leader or follower? I don't think so.

The days of the judgmental leader should be left in the past. I once wrote an article about divorcing the past. It's time to divorce the past.

- Divorce the past of judging
- Divorce the past of not caring
- Divorce the past of lack of valuing followers
- Divorce the past of only being results oriented
- Divorce the past of only having a self-interest

Don't get caught up in the stereotype of being a BOSS. In the past, we have typically referred to leaders as bosses. But in today's world, we need leaders instead of bosses. No more finger pointing! We can look back on the history of leadership and learn what the true results of having bosses can be. They may include:

1. Fear as already stated
2. Lack of team member independence
3. Sterile culture
4. High turnover

Is this what leaders hope for? I propose that we should all be focusing on how to combat these very issues. These components are not conducive to how we want to achieve success.

Maybe this has been an effective style of leadership in the past and produced great results. We must realize that times change, generations change, and the past should only provide us lessons and can't be lived in. One of my mentors, Bob Padalino, once told me, "Jeff, you can't drive a car looking in the rearview mirror." It's time to look forward and be willing to change for the good of those you lead. Society is experiencing a shift! Today, "the combination of globalization and new, differently manageable generations coming into the workforce is creating the need for new kinds of leadership,"[2] writes Brent Filson. In my experience, I have found that employees are looking for a leader they can relate to and feel comfortable in being able to approach. They are searching for a leader who is different from those they have followed in the past. This leader must establish and build relationships with the employees and prove they are truly valued in the organization.

Employees can easily identify judgmental leaders. These leaders tend to have an attitude that if the employees do not like their decisions, they can leave the organization. They have a knee-jerk reaction to any unpleasant situation, and that response can sometimes have its place if a quick decision is required. However, we should not routinely be leaders who do not allow input regarding our decisions. It's not about us, but it's about using our leadership roles to help others. We cannot forget who is in the organization and how we can benefit them. Without followers, there is no one to lead! Without employees, there will not be an organization!

If a judgmental leader does not allow input from staff and he/she leads based on self-interest, then long-term failure can be the only expected result. I understand we can't negate the fact that results need to be achieved. These results are directly related to a leader's style. Power is no longer the sole cause for producing influence; therefore, sustainable results are not guaranteed.

I once thought employees wanted to be productive based on their own personal values, but as I have progressed throughout my career, I feel somewhat differently. Through my observations, I have found that people do have sincerity about them to do a good job in their specific roles. But I have discovered that if they are serving under a judgmental leader, the focus shifts from the value of doing a good job to the environment to which they are subjected. They still want to perform their responsibilities, but they question whether they want to perform these duties effectively for their leader. Let me present the following scenario for consideration.

A director (judgmental leader) is told about an employee who is not pulling his weight. Other employees continually tell the director of performance issues regarding the employee, but the director becomes aggravated with the constant complaints. He does not address the issue, and the situation becomes exacerbated. The employees are now frustrated, so their productivity becomes less. They do not see any reason to perform at a certain level because their coworker is not forced to fulfill his responsibilities. The director does not take the time to listen. He becomes frustrated because the employees are complaining, and because of his frustration, he does not address the situation. What happens? Productivity within the department decreases, and conflict arises between the leadership and staff and also among the staff members. These are good employees who value their roles and responsibilities, but they are frustrated because the leader does not seem to value them and is not holding the low-performing employee accountable to fulfill his responsibilities.

The question arises, "Is there a choice?" If judgmental leadership impacts the followers negatively, what is the alternative? I believe the alternative is merciful leadership. It is demonstrated by the following characteristics: forgiveness, love, compassion, understanding, humility, service, courage, and commitment.

As we progress through the characteristics of a mercy leader, think about how this paradigm would likely increase employee productivity. When thinking about this comparison and how it can relate to productivity, we should look beyond mere theoretical observations. Instead, we must dive into the realm of common sense. As a follower, I am more productive for a leader who truly values me as such, but I find it more of a struggle to be productive for a leader who prefers a domineering style of leadership and values me only as a number within the organization. As a leader, I prefer to show my followers I care for them, and I truly believe my focus should be on developing them. Through my actions, I hope they will be more productive as well as develop both professionally and personally.

Mercy leaders can present a more positive impact within organizations as well as in the lives of people. We are not only in the organization business, but we are in the people business! What benefit do we have by being more merciful to our followers? We create an atmosphere of unity that will provide a more productive organization. The first characteristic of a merciful leader is to be forgiving. I started with characteristic because this is the very foundation and uniqueness of a mercy leader. You may study all different methods of leadership but this defining characteristic is the foundation of a mercy leader.

TIME FOR REFLECTION—ARE YOU A MERCY LEADER?

1. How do you treat others?
2. Do you truly value others in your organization?
3. Do you have a tendency to rush to judgment?

Each of these questions is very important when considering your interactions with others. As you explore each characteristic of a mercy leader, use the time for reflection found at the end of each chapter to reflect on your leadership method.

CHAPTER 2
MERCY LEADERS FORGIVE

"O man, forgive thy mortal foe

Nor ever strike him blow for blow,

For all the saints on earth that live

To be forgiven must forgive,

For all the blessed souls in heaven

Are both forgivers and forgiven."[3]

At first glance, this characteristic seems to be at odds with leadership. Why should we be forgiving? Too many times forgiveness is seen as weakness, but I have personally been on the receiving end of forgiveness and found it to be life changing.

In 2006, I was assigned the task of negotiating a contract for biomedical services for one of my previous employers. During this process, a decision was made to contract with a specific company, and I gave notice to the vendor, who was our current supplier, their services would no longer be needed. When I gave notice to the vendor, I intended to keep the service contracts only on specific radiology equipment. Unfortunately, canceling the equipment contract also canceled the service contract on these specific pieces. Naturally, I didn't realize this until the CT scanner at the sister hospital experienced problems, and we found out there was no service to be had. The repairs required were not worth the value of the CT scanner, and we were forced to buy a new one. This resulted in a significant expense that was not budgeted, which is always a bad thing. I was devastated by this costly mistake and expected some disciplinary action. I immediately went to my CEO, David Fuqua, and apologized for this error.

Instead of discipline, I was extended forgiveness. During this time of agony, frustration, and beating myself up mentally, forgiveness was granted. This defining moment forever changed my perspective on the influence of leadership. It wasn't some lip-service extended to me, but it was an action. We have all known people who said they forgave us, but then they treated us differently or held a grudge against us. My CEO was not this way. He didn't forgive me and then talk about me in a negative manner to others. He completely forgave me and used the opportunity to discuss the situation and how we could prevent a similar situation moving forward. I definitely learned from my mistake. I personally found that forgiveness is both inspirational and life changing. My CEO knew I was a leader with limited experience and would make mistakes, and he was willing to show me merciful leadership by forgiving my mistake and allowing me to learn from it. He was a true mercy leader in the way he treated me.

I remember seeing an illustration from a hospital chaplain that exemplifies forgiveness. He had a bowl of water that represented the world before sin. The chaplain put a white handkerchief into the water and showed it to the people in the room. Of course, the handkerchief was white and represented the world. After removing the handkerchief, he then took a bottle labeled sin which contained a chemical. When he poured the chemical into the water, the water became dark brown. He then put the handkerchief into the brown water, and it became brown, representing our lives before experiencing forgiveness from Christ.

A second bowl represented Christ and His forgiveness. This bowl contained water with a clear chemical. The chaplain placed the handkerchief into the second bowl, and it immediately became white again showing the power of Christ's forgiveness and how He can clean us up. The chaplain then placed the handkerchief into the first bowl, and the brown chemical cleared up. This represented the power of Christ's forgiveness and how His forgiveness can clean up the sins of the world.

You may question how this simple example can impact you and your organization. In the context of an organization, the internal environment can easily become troubled and morale can decrease. This leads to retention issues and increased customer grievances. Ultimately, the organization's financial bottom line is negatively impacted. Let's look at this example when considering a troubled organization.

When an organization grows and employees are hired, human issues creep into the environment, causing internal turmoil.

Instead of focusing on the results, a strong, merciful leader is focused on the employees, and the organization is sensitive to these issues. Forgiveness is shown in these times by not overlooking the issues but finding the reasons for them. A mercy leader then collaborates with the followers to fix the issues. Now the followers feel valued and the organization produces the expected results. Merciful leadership truly impacts the culture of the organization. Tolerance is spawned. Employees find themselves more willing to forgive each other and you! However, if the leader does not value the employees, both the employees and the organization will be impacted in the opposite way. Minor problems become larger. Personal problems become organizational problems, and the leader gets the blame from all sides.

L. B. Jones writes, "Forgiveness is like oil in an engine. It keeps the wheels moving. Forgiveness is like gravity . . . invisible in its power yet profound in its effects."[4] This is a powerful statement to the impact of forgiveness. So, the question turns to what it is we should forgive. Should all behaviors be forgiven? Should we treat failure and laziness (lack of work ethic) as equals? After all, the consequences of both are the same: Things don't get done. I say, "No." A lack of work ethic equates to a lack of drive. It is something an organization cannot afford to support and will spell the doom of any leader or company that allows it to foster. Failure is much less an offense than apathy. In fact, some people believe failure should be rewarded because it means people are willing to try different options and willing to fail. Failures can be viewed as a learning tool. Innovative people in our history did not see failures as failing but rather as opportunities to create more ideas. The founder of the Johnson and Johnson Company once declared, "If I wasn't making mistakes, I wasn't making decisions."[5] Obviously, he realized people make mistakes. It is this realization and understanding that can assist leaders in developing the ability to forgive others. "Forgiveness does not mean being a doormat or not using discretion in whom you deal with and how. Forgiveness means allowing others to make mistakes while you and they keep moving forward."[6]

My favorite example of forgiveness was shown by Jesus Christ. Jesus had been teaching people in the Temple, and the scribes and Pharisees approached Him. They brought a woman who had been caught in the act of adultery. During their testing of Christ, the scribes and Pharisees referred to the Law of Moses that called for a punishment of stoning for this type of act. Jesus told them, "He who is without sin among you, let him throw a stone at her first" (John 8:7, NKJV). Each of the accusers was "convicted by their conscience" and left (John 8:9, NKJV). Jesus asked the woman where her accusers had gone and if any one of them had condemned her. She stated that not even one of them had condemned her, and Jesus said, "Neither do I condemn you; go, and from now on sin no more" (John 8:11, ESV). The scribes and Pharisees were quick to judge the woman. However, when Jesus reminded them they had also sinned, they were no longer able to condemn her. Jesus exemplified forgiveness by not condemning her sin but showed mercy and instructed for her to sin no more.

What would happen if you looked at your follower and extended forgiveness even when it may not be popular? I know that it would make a significant impact in that person's life and would allow him or her another chance to make a positive impact in the organization. Not only does it make an impact on the organization, but you have now invested into their career journey and lives. I will always carry with me the act of forgiveness shown by leaders in my journey, and it will forever make a positive impact on my career and life.

We also see here one of the problems with people in a leadership role. They forget where they came from. In the shared biblical account, the judgmental leaders did not focus on the times they had made mistakes. They wanted to point a finger at the accused and "write her off" with their judgement. However, when reminded of their mistakes, their attitudes changed. Before judging others, remember where you have been and the mistakes you have made. This has been an important component for me as a leader. I know I have made mistakes and will continue to make them. I try to be mindful of this when dealing with others who make mistakes.

Of course, all this requires a willingness to forgive others. As human beings, it is often our first instinct to blame. You may be following the example of every boss you have ever had who was quite willing to treat mistakes like the end of the world. Forgiveness was a sign of weakness to these kinds of people, so maybe it would help if we defined forgiveness at this point. Forgiving does not mean you ignore the mistakes. When an employee makes a mistake, it would be foolish to act as if it had never happened since the severity of this mistake can impact the organization. I would also be foolish if I did not take the time to find out why the mistake happened. Are the employees over their heads? Do they care about the job they are doing, or was it a momentary lapse in judgment? My point is, we cannot be too quick to judge without considering all aspects of the issue and attempting to develop our employees if possible. These snap judgments can hurt us by robbing our organization of employees with great potential, hindering their ability to learn from their mistakes. "Learning without facing some chance of failure is superficial progress, not real change."[7] By promoting a forgiving atmosphere, you allow people to take chances and use creative thinking.

Encourage other leaders that are part of your journey to be forgiving, to develop others, and to value their followers. Be examples by extending forgiveness to others. Forgiveness is not only for front-line staff members, but also forgiveness should be shown to other leaders. Throughout my career, I have heard that the higher up in the "food chain," the harder the ax falls. As individuals progress in their leadership roles, they are quicker to be judged like they are non-essential. This thought is very disturbing to me. Why do we not realize leaders make mistakes and may also need developing? I have heard stories about leaders being terminated for no true cause. It could simply be they rub someone the wrong way. This is not fair to the leadership within the organization. A culture of forgiveness fosters creative and impactful leaders!

Of course, developing a forgiving heart takes time. If you are reading this and have never heard of forgiveness in leadership, please know this characteristic may take time to implement into your leadership journey and does not happen overnight. It is a process, and requires a love for those you lead.

TIME FOR REFLECTION—FORGIVENESS

1. Do you forgive others when they make mistakes?
2. Do you invest time in determining why employees make repeated mistakes?
3. Do you encourage others in the organization to forgive?

This characteristic was listed first because of its profound impact on others. Take a moment to reflect on a time you were shown forgiveness. How did this action make you feel? If you have not been on the receiving end, I encourage you to be on the giving end. The response is just as profound in comparison.

CHAPTER 3
MERCY LEADERS LOVE

"Love and kindness are never wasted. They always make a difference. They bless the one who receives them, and they bless you, the giver."[8]

—Barbara De Angelis

According to Laurie Beth Jones, "Love is the infrastructure of everything and anything worthwhile."[9] This component of leadership may sound too soft and fluffy to some leaders and even reading this chapter may stir a sense of being uncomfortable. I firmly believe that before we can forgive others and show people mercy, we must love them with a moral love. The Greeks called it *agapao* love.[10] This word refers to doing the right thing at the right time for the right reason. More specifically, *agapao* means to love in a "social or moral sense, embracing the judgment and the deliberate assent of the will as a matter of principle, duty and propriety."[11] To me, the question is, How can people effectively lead others if they don't love them? If you lead others, it is your duty to love them. Loving them does not require that you know everything about them. We can safely assume that leaders of large companies do not know every one of their employees. This does not mean you kiss and hug all of your followers. (This may get you into trouble in today's world and be a HR issue). However, it does mean you

DR. JEFFREY A. RADFORD

are able to look over the superficial layer of labeling them only as a follower and instead consider them as a human being. You cease to see them as an asset and begin to view them as a person. We all know that nobody is perfect. As a leader and as a person, you have made and will make mistakes. The love I am advocating here is one that realizes the simple fact that perfection cannot be achieved, only aspired to. Your followers are grappling with the realities of everyday life. They face tough situations while also trying to perform at work. Mercy leaders show love to others as they face struggles, and we help them develop and make it through those struggles. Determine if you love your employees and be willing to transform yourself as you develop a strong love for them.

I know! You are reading this chapter and struggling with the word "love" and "follower" in the same context. It's something that is not taught in the business administration textbook. It doesn't seem to flow well in the same context of a leader. Maybe it goes against what you have experienced or envisioned. However, if you are willing to be a mercy leader and practice forgiveness, the action of love is essential.

There is an alternative to love. The antonym for love is hate. In an organizational context, what would the organization be like if more love than hate existed? First, look at what hate does to an organization. Hate leads to dissension, and dissension leads to a lack of uniformity. Where there is dissension, goals are missed, projects fall apart, and generally nothing gets done.

As a leader for several years now, I am well aware of the arguing and negative attitudes of people that sometimes exist within organizations and sometimes among leaders. Arguments start because of simple issues, instead of looking at the "why" or having the ability to look beyond self-interests and focus on common organizational goals. We are sometimes so blind to our own self-interests that we forget to look at other things that should grasp our attention. If we spent more time loving each other, a concern would grow, and our actions would blossom to show that person our love for them.

If love is shown, the small irritating things we all do as human beings are smoothed down until they do not irritate at all. Love sometimes requires discipline so the person realizes he/she has done wrong. For example, I love my children with all my heart, and I know my wife loves our children deeply as well. This love for them does not take away the responsibility to teach them when they do wrong. We discipline our children because we love them. The discipline teaches them to remember they have done wrong, and we hope they will learn not to repeat the same mistake. At times, we discipline our followers to help them realize they have made a mistake, so they remember their wrong and try not to repeat the mistake.

Martin Luther King, Jr. once said, "Whom you would change, you must first love."[12] This is an excellent quote that exemplifies my point. If you want others to learn and grow from their mistakes, you must first love them. You will want them to change, not out of self-interest, but out of a love for them that will want them to succeed and develop. If we all loved each other, our world would be a different place! It might actually become a place where we could unite together to make a positive impact.

This love makes you want to restore the fallen. Billy Graham was well known for loving others. He was internationally respected for the love shown to countless people. Jim Bakker, during and after the prison time he served for mistakes he made, experienced this love from Billy and Ruth Graham. During Bakker's imprisonment, the Grahams maintained their friendship with him. After Bakker served his prison time, the Grahams "paid for a house for him to live in and provided him a car."[13] His legacy is known for loving others, and although I did not know Billy Graham personally, I sensed an authenticity about his character. Followers sense the authenticity of their leader's love, and they will bond to that leader. If you want your followers to follow you, show them you truly love them. Your love will be exemplified by your actions.

Mercy is a result of this action and love. Do not let your heart harden toward those you lead. I understand we can become weary from day-to-day problems that require our input and decision-making. Some followers constantly require our attention and seem to become a drain. At times, we feel as if we have no one who understands what we as leaders experience; therefore, we feel as if we have no one to talk to. Have you ever felt loneliness in your leadership role? I have felt isolated in my leadership role without anyone to talk to. However, the reward that comes from showing love to others is a true benefit of the leadership role.

Love requires action, and we should love one another. Love is not a feeling, and it demands demonstration. At one of my leadership meetings, I told my team that I loved them. They are familiar with my leadership so it did not create a "shock" within the room. I was not afraid to say it and it was sincere. However, this statement went beyond words. What is your response when you hear an employee was sick or experienced a death in the family or was struggling through some type of issue? Do you make an effort to talk with them and ask them how they are doing? This shows love for them. This love will cause leaders to show others they are valued in their roles. The intent of my heart is to show others I truly love them and value them as a person and a follower. My experience shows a reciprocal effect of love being given back.

We can attend every meeting and give wonderful speeches about how we value the employees, and to some that will mean something. When you show love in your actions, employees will positively respond. "Love is patient, love is kind, it is not puffed up or arrogant (humble), it does not act unbecomingly (respectful), it does not seek its own (selfless), it does not take into account a wrong suffered (forgiving), it does not rejoice in unrighteousness but rejoices in the truth (honest), it bears all things, endures all things, it never fails (committed)."[14]

Some may find this action to be difficult because the employee is difficult to deal with. C. S. Lewis once remarked, "Do not waste time bothering whether you 'love' your neighbor; act as if you did. As soon as we do this, we find one of the great secrets. When you are behaving as if you love someone, you will presently come to love him."[15]

The best advice I can give leaders is that when you feel you cannot love someone, do it anyway. Show loving actions toward them. Some of the employees may have had a bad past, and you might never realize the impact of loving actions toward them. When I managed an orthopedic practice, one of the most important issues I focused on was showing loving actions to our customers. I informed the staff that we would never know the impact of our actions toward the customers. We do not know what a child or a spouse might be experiencing at home. This is true when you relate to your employees. Some of the only loving actions they receive may be the actions you show them. This love will lead to mercy. Be merciful to your followers, and not only will you benefit the employee, but you will also feel better about yourself. When being genuine with your loving actions, the result will lead to compassion for others.

TIME FOR REFLECTION—LOVE

1. Do you love your employees?
2. Is this love superficial, or do you truly seek to nurture and develop your employees?
3. Is your love shown through actions?

Love is shown through actions. As you reflect on this characteristic, determine if you love and value your employees. If so, you must ensure that you show your love through actions. As you communicate this love, encourage others within the organization to "love one another."

CHAPTER 4
MERCY LEADERS HAVE COMPASSION

"Until he extends the circle of compassion, man will not himself find peace"[16]

—Albert Schwietzer.

By loving others, we develop a compassion for them. By compassion, I mean the ability to put ourselves in their shoes, to be sympathetic to . . . (1) who they are and (2) what they are going through. It is a step of becoming a mercy leader that takes us beyond love as an idea and into a more concrete practice. As leaders, we must have compassion for everyone within the organization. There are times that I deal with people and their actions that cause me to become frustrated, but I must realize that I cannot cut them off and show compassion to everyone BUT them. Our compassion for others will cause us to be merciful towards them. This caring attitude will create a caring atmosphere.

Caring begins with the heart. The heart must be prepared by a genuine love for others. This preparation will ready the heart for an action of caring. According to Perry Pascarella, "Building caring relationships is not a matter of determining which techniques to implement or which practices to avoid. It begins in the heart and will, and then cascades outward in caring for other persons."[17]

When leaders show compassion and mercy, they make it more likely that they will in return receive compassion and mercy. "Blessed is the leader who shows compassion and mercy to the people who work with him, for his employees show him an equal amount of compassion and mercy."[18] As with love and forgiveness, you will find that by showing compassion for others. You will receive compassion, not always, but more often than if you are not compassionate. When I worked as a nurse, there were many times that I did not receive the same compassion that I had shown to patients and their families. However, a simple thank you, though it was infrequent, seemed to help me during my lowest times in that role. There are times, and there will continue to be times, that being a leader will seem to be a thankless position. However, if you have compassion for others, you will have a drive to want to better their lives.

How many times do you put out the fires of complaints from followers? How many times do people come to you to fix all of the issues? It almost becomes habitual because the leader is the one that fixes it all. However, the number of times of solving issues does not equate to the number of times gratitude is shown by those who bring the issues.

Let me challenge you. We should not be in the leadership role for the thank you. To be more specific, it is not about us. I will be the first to raise my hand and say gratitude from others helps provide me an energy to keep going. I must also point out that if I only relied on the gratitude, my energy level would remain very low. What other means are you tapping into to keep the energy at a high level? So far, the chapters you have read require action and action requires energy. Compassion is no different and is equally important in your leadership journey.

The ability to be compassionate helps us show mercy to others.

Misericordia, the word tells it, *miseria cordis, miserum cor*, is a heart accessible to the miserable. St. Thomas defines it thus: A compassion which constrains our soul at the sight of the misery of another and urges us to succor him to the measure of our ability. It makes us enter into the misfortune of others and share in it in making it our own. With those who suffer and who weep, we suffer and weep; the echo of all their sorrows resounds in our heart. This is but one phase of mercy, its minor aspect; nevertheless, a precious one, for it is not a small thing to have a compassionate and sincere friend in time of trial.[19]

Sympathy is worth more than what people will be able to express to you. The compassion I have experienced from others seldom can be explained in simple words, but I know its impact. I also know that when I show compassion to others, it makes a difference. According to Christine Zust, "We have spent decades becoming more professional and businesslike, and in the process we have built impenetrable armor around ourselves."[20] I am certain there will continue to be leaders who are results driven instead of people driven, but "we may find that those who exhibit the characteristics of a compassionate leader will fare better in handling crises and communicating more effectively in any economic and social climate."[21]

As a leader, what do you care about? If you care about your followers, you will gain positive results. If you care more about results, you will lose your followers and most likely experience their going away from the mission of the organization. The success will come if the intent of the organization is to care about your people. Mercy is shown because you care for others.

In my past experience, I had a department director with two significant employee issues. In the first scenario, this department director had an employee who had constant counseling due to performance issues. The employee continued to fail to respond to the counseling, and I became frustrated with the employee's performance. This lack of performance was impacting the organization and also the department. Although frustrated, I understood that I needed to allow the department director to address the situation. This would allow him to grow in his role as long as the organization was not severely impacted. Although I had my doubts about the employee's ability to improve, the director invested time in finding the reasons for the performance issues, and to my surprise, the employee did significantly improve.

In another scenario, a department director had an employee transfer into his department who could not seem to grasp the responsibilities of the role. During the initial 90-day trial period, the employee continued to lack the ability to fulfill the responsibilities of the position. However, this director cared about the employee and found other positive characteristics, which included dependability and an excellent character. Because of these positive characteristics, he invested the time to intensely train the employee and extend the trial period. This employee went on to perform the responsibilities of the position and proved to be valuable to the department.

In both scenarios, why did the director invest the time to determine how to improve the employee's performance? Because there was a sincere compassion for these employees, time was allowed, and this time proved to be well spent. In my leadership role during these scenarios, I cared about the director and allowed this person the autonomy to address the issues. We all developed through these experiences, and I found, as a result, we now have two very valuable employees.

However, sometimes being compassionate to an employee means knowing when it is time to sever the relationship between the employee and the company. If the job is not right for them or if it causes more stress to the employee and the company environment, then the compassionate thing to do is remove the person. In the long run, it is better for both the individual and the company. The trick is to know the differences in these situations. You can lead with your heart but use your mind to discern what is right.

Nothing is easy about disciplining employees or terminating employees. However, I have found that most of the time, the employees usually terminate themselves because even if we provide opportunities for them to improve, they may continue on a downhill slide. If I have invested time to develop these employees and they continue to perform poorly, then they have terminated themselves, and I have to follow the proper procedures to finish the termination or advance the disciplinary process.

We never stop learning to properly show compassion. I am not a perfect leader and never will claim to be. I continually self-reflect about how I can handle situations differently to show mercy to others. I do not want to lead based on caring about myself, but rather, I want to lead based on caring about others. Times occur when we must make tough decisions. However, if we have made those decisions with both our hearts and minds and have attempted to do the right thing for both the employee and organization, we can rest assured that we approached the situation with a caring and compassionate attitude. Caring that much will make us attempt to understand those whom we are leading.

TIME FOR REFLECTION—COMPASSION

1. Do you have compassion for your employees?
2. Do you attempt to put yourself in your employees' shoes?
3. Is your compassion shown through your actions?

As with love, compassion should be shown through actions. By fostering an atmosphere of compassion, you encourage others to have this action as well. Love will lead to compassion. Compassion leads to forgiveness and you will find that as a leader, you are well on your way to being a mercy leader.

CHAPTER 5
MERCY LEADERS UNDERSTAND

"Happy is the man who finds wisdom, and the man who gets understanding."

— Proverbs 3:13, NLV

"Leadership should be born out of the understanding of the needs of those who would be affected by it." [22]

—Marian Anderson

W hy do we need understanding? I think the above quote from Marian Anderson explains it best. We can become more effective leaders by understanding those we lead. This is also an important component of merciful leadership. To be a mercy leader, how can we show mercy if we don't attempt to understand why or to whom we are showing mercy to? Here is another actionable requirement. To show mercy you must first seek to understand. Now I do not claim to know everything—there is always room to learn—but the drive to learn and understand helps us discern when to show mercy and when to show justice. For example, I have shown mercy multiple times in my career, and I have come to understand that some employees will not improve. Consequently, through disciplinary actions, they have left the organization.

One type of understanding is when a leader attempts to be sympathetic or considerate of others. We have already discussed this kind of compassionate understanding. A mercy leader attempts to show this understanding or sympathy when an employee does something wrong, is suffering in the workplace, and so on, but there is another type of understanding. Here the term means having perception. This perception is absolutely necessary when attempting to discern when mercy should be shown by exhibiting disciplinary actions.

When I graduated from nursing school, I was given information from my education about treatment of specific disease processes. But I did not fully understand my role as a nurse. Only when I started working as a nurse did I begin to understand. Only when I interacted with the people in my care did I see that nursing was much more than facts in a book. It required people skills, discernment, and more than a little patience. Even that did not cover all there was to being a nurse.

This is also true in my role as a leader. In the beginning of my first leadership role, I was "green as grass." I managed an orthopedic clinic with fourteen employees and didn't have a clue about the responsibilities of my role. I was three months away from obtaining my master of business administration degree. I was obtaining an education but did not yet have understanding. Education is very important, but people get into a trap of believing that once they have a degree, they are ready for their roles. It is this mentality that will quickly lead you down the path to failure.

My first position as a registered nurse (RN) was on a medical/surgical floor working night shift in a hospital. I could easily have had a know-it-all mentality because I was a RN and some of the other staff members were not, but if I had that mentality, failure would have been my ultimate demise. I learned to surround myself with others who had their education and understanding because of their experience, and I credit them for helping me develop as a nurse. Just because people are placed under you on an organizational chart does not mean they can't teach you something about your job. As leaders, we have to understand that some of our followers can actually help us develop in our leadership roles. My mentor told me he often surrounded himself with people smarter than he was to make him look smart. He was not intimidated, but rather he welcomed those people to help him develop in his role.

Our mentality of being intimidated by our followers has to go away. If I knew everything about the departments I'm responsible for, I wouldn't need leaders in those departments. I need those leaders to help me understand the departments, and I rely on the employees in those departments for understanding.

Of course, we should also look at our own personal experiences to help us gain understanding about those we lead. We are all human. We know what it is like to have human problems. For example, family issues have sometimes caused me to leave work early or even miss work. This helps me understand that my employees will at times have family issues.

As leaders, we should understand there is also a reciprocal impact by the way we treat others. So far, we have been focused on understanding others and how this characteristic helps us show mercy to our followers. However, another component of understanding, is to understand the impact of our actions on our followers and on us. Richard Daft wrote, "Leaders must remember that every statement and action has an impact on culture and values, perhaps without their realizing it."[23] Being merciful runs both ways—not every time, but in general. Hopefully as a leader, you set a good example by showing understanding and mercy. If so, when your employees are in a position to do so, they will show you mercy and all the characteristics we have studied so far.

Our effort to understand others also encompasses attempting to understand their values. This effort allows leaders to be more effective, because they seek to understand the values of their followers and make every attempt to avoid breaking them when possible.[24] Is the reason for poor performance of the employee due to a lack of alignment of the employee's values with the organization's values? If so, what can be done to ensure these values align in the future? This also requires us to communicate our values and the organization's values to employees, so they can have a better understanding of leadership, the organization, and our focus.

Understanding also requires the leader to take time to listen to employees and learn about issues that are important to them. Listening "is not just keeping still, or even remembering what is said. Listening is an attitude, an attitude toward other people and what they are trying to express. It begins with a genuine interest that is manifest in close attention, and it goes on to understanding in depth—whence cometh wisdom."[25] Day-to-day operations can be very time consuming and cause us to seemingly be stuck in our offices instead of spending time with the employees. However, don't let the day-to-day get in the way of spending time with those that ultimately make you successful as a leader.

When I was working on the medical/surgical floor, I always felt important when the CEO of the hospital would take time from his day to come to my work area and ask me about my day and how I was doing. I felt as if he were attempting to understand me and my role. During my other leadership roles, I have found the level of leadership engagement directly impacts the culture of those being led. A balance must be struck: making rounds within our organization, greeting employees and learning their issues, and spending time in the office to address those issues. Do this with genuine interest. In the past, I have known leaders who made rounds to meet employees but gave empty promises to make them look good in the eyes of the employees. They didn't fool anyone.

On the other end of the spectrum, I have known leaders who rarely visited the departments, and employees complained that they never saw the CEO. I feel they missed that personal connection. Employees are watching the actions of a leader. We lead, not only by giving direction, but also by our actions. "There is an old saying in leadership circles that everything the leader does sends a message."[26] If you truly intend to understand employees and spend time with them, they will be able to bond with you and understand you.

President Abraham Lincoln relieved General John C. Fremont from his command in Missouri on September 9, 1861. His reasoning was that General Fremont's "cardinal mistake is that he isolates himself, and allows nobody to see him; and by which he does not know what is going on in the very matter he is dealing with."[27] President Lincoln realized he would have to circulate among those he led to understand them. This understanding would assist him in his decision-making and leadership. He was very involved as a president. He spent a great deal of time at the Department of War's telegraph office so he could gain access to key information to assist him in making quick and timely decisions.[28] He continually met with his leaders and other key individuals in the government. President Lincoln's personal secretaries "reported that Lincoln spent 75 percent of his time meeting with people."[29] I don't know that today we could get a lot accomplished if we met with people 75 percent of our time. However, the point is, that to gain knowledge and understanding, we have to be in touch with our employees.

One problem is that our self wants to get in the way and sometimes not show mercy. Self will want us to focus the attention on what *we* are doing for the organization. This desire can be detrimental. I once wrote an article about a great decision not always being the right decision. Instead of searching for the great decision that may elevate us in our career and look good on the resume, we should remove self and determine the right decision based on our understanding. This removing of self requires us to have humility.

TIME FOR REFLECTION—UNDERSTANDING

1. Do you invest the time to understand your employees?
2. Do you communicate effectively with employees within the organization to allow them the opportunity to understand you?
3. Do you encourage others within the organization to invest time in understanding others?

Gaining understanding allows us to determine when we should apply mercy to a situation. We can all obtain advanced education and attend seminars that teach about leadership. These allow us to have wisdom but not necessarily understanding. This will come from two key components: a willingness to seek to understand others and an investment in taking the time to understand others.

CHAPTER 6
MERCIFUL LEADERS ARE HUMBLE

"For whoever exalts himself will be humbled, and whoever humbles himself will be exalted."

—Matthew 23:12, NIV

"It is unwise to be too sure of one's own wisdom. It is healthy to be reminded that the strongest might weaken and the wisest may err."[30]

—Mohandis K. Ghandi

O ur willingness to practice humility will be the gateway to showing mercy to others. There is a scripture in the Bible that points to those who are humble will be exalted. This means taking the focus off you. Your primary goal is not the advancement of your ego. Instead, you are focused on the organization you serve and the followers who depend on you to make decisions.

During the beginning of my doctoral program, I was struggling. I went to a professor and explained that I did not feel I should be in the education program based on the students I had met and their qualifications versus mine. These students used words I did not understand and probably could not even spell. It was a sense of inadequacy and being under-qualified. The professor told me something I grabbed onto and will always remember. He told me that some of those students would not finish the program because they were not willing to learn. The key to finishing the program was to have a willingness to learn and to have endurance. As I approached the end of the program, his statement turned out to be true. The key for me was to be humble, to be willing to learn, and to endure to the end. I could not do it on my own. I give credit to God who allowed me to have the strength to finish.

Now I have not always been humble in my life. To be honest, I'm not always as humble as I could be. When the desire to promote self begins to sneak in, I try to pay attention. In my career goals, I once wanted to be the CEO because I considered this the top position in health care. I wanted to obtain my doctorate degree because it was the top degree. I wanted to make a lot of money and obtain success. Self was the overriding focus. As a result, I have done things that were in my own best interest, not in the best interests of those around me.

I'm not saying people should not have goals or strive to achieve those goals. My point is to look at the reasoning for those goals. I still want to be in a top leadership role, but now I want it because I believe it will allow me to help more people. I want to be successful, but my reasons have drastically changed. When the reasons changed, the results were very different, and the stress of self-promotion was eased.

According to Jerry Wofford, "Humility is a strange attribute. The moment you ask yourself if you have it, you lose it. When you reach out to take hold of it, you push it farther away. You cannot gain a humble attitude by attempting to become humble because the attempt turns your eyes back on yourself. Like love, humility grows out of service to others in obedience to God."[31]

Referring to my own experience of making it through my educational program, I was willing to learn more. I didn't know it all and was teachable! I recall reflecting on this while standing alone during my hooding ceremony at the completion of my doctoral program. I surveyed the room and the words of endurance and a willingness to learn came to my mind. Be humble and enjoy the journey of learning. Have endurance to navigate this leadership journey. Be willing to extend mercy. When being merciful, we are not only benefiting others, but we are also learning more from the situation. Being a humble leader can also be defined as being poor in spirit. "The leader who is poor in spirit knows that his employees are intelligent people who, many times, know more of the details of the job and thus have worthwhile advice to give. This is a key premise of total quality leadership—to teach the employees how to solve problems, develop solutions, and then trust them to do the work. A humble leader does not lord over his employees or force answers and solutions upon them."[32]

An example of humility can be found when reading about Joseph in the Bible. It is a striking story. "God strategically positioned this humble man as king over Egypt at a crucial time in world history," John Maxwell notes. "When nightmares awakened Pharaoh, he recognized something odd was happening. As a strong leader he acknowledged his sense of unease, but as a humble leader he enlisted the advice of others."[33]

He had enlisted the help of a man named Joseph, who was able to interpret Pharaoh's dreams. Joseph was rewarded for correctly interpreting the dreams, and because the king listened to Joseph, many lives were saved from starvation. "Pharaoh listened carefully, empowered Joseph to act," Maxwell continues, "and in so doing, ensured his own legacy as an effective leader."[34] With this great example, a leader can be inspired to include the act of humility in his/her leadership style. I don't know about you, but when I hear stories about men of significant influence realizing they still have things to learn, I come away impressed.

Referring to my previous point about a leader compared to a boss, I visualize a boss as not being humble. One who thrives on power and self-gratitude. The boss creates fear, and his followers are intimidated by his character. As leaders, do not expect your people to be afraid of you. If your employees fear you as a leader, your organization will lack creativity and innovation because they will be afraid to help you grow and develop the organization.

It is also essential to engage followers through an open-door policy or rounding. Have you ever worked for a leader who wants you to know he/she is your boss? Every time you want to talk with your boss, you have to schedule an appointment. You are limited to a specific amount of time, and you may even have to provide a detailed outline of what you want to talk about. This may be an attempt to be prepared for the meeting, but more likely it is a way to control the meeting. I have worked for leaders who wanted full control, but I have also worked for leaders who have an open-door policy and encourage people to communicate with them. If you do not communicate with others, you will be limited in the information you have to make appropriate decisions.

According to Dr. Bruce Winston, a humble leader will show respect to everyone in the workplace.[35] The ability to show respect makes a great impact on others. Humility is never a sign of weakness nor is it a mark of a lack of self-respect or low self-esteem.[36] Humility fights against believing yourself more able than you actually are or developing a sense of self-entitlement. Humility is a characteristic that keeps you in check as a person and a leader.

It is a realization that although you may be the top dog in your organization, you should use that position to help your organization and those you lead. The top dog role is not an opportunity to boast about your position and control others. Some of the leaders of the biggest corporations have fallen because they started focusing on themselves instead of focusing on how they could use their role to help the organization. On the other hand, some of the most successful leaders succeed because they are humble. In the context of leadership, a humble leader will inherit the respect of those he/she leads because they truly want to serve others.

TIME FOR REFLECTION—HUMILITY

1. When making decisions, do you make them out of self-interest, or do you consider the impact on the organization?
2. Do you use your position to help others climb the career ladder?

3. Are you willing to allow others to have input when making decisions?

Merciful leadership requires a leader to remove self-interest and be willing to show mercy to others. When considering forgiveness, love, compassion, and understanding, the characteristic of humility is required. Why? Because before you can have those four characteristics for others, humility is required to remove self. At times, self does not want to forgive others, love others, have compassion for others, or understand others, but humility will allow a gateway for the other characteristics and allow you to show mercy.

CHAPTER 7
MERCIFUL LEADERS SERVE

"Good leaders must first become good servants."[37]

—Robert Greenleaf

Robert Greenleaf, who introduced the term "servant leader,"[38] believed a component of good leadership is being a servant to those whom one leads. This may seem to be conflicting. How can you serve someone if you are leading that person? You must develop a servant mentality. By becoming a servant, a leader uses the leadership position to serve the needs of the employees. In the past, my fellow employees have kidded me that I am in the "white house," a term used for the administration offices. One employee defined my role by saying I was "one of them." I still wonder why that person would classify administrative staff as "them" as if some type of separation existed. (There may be a natural separation, but this is because of the different responsibilities associated with each position. My goal is to have administration viewed more as someone who is on the same team as the employees to accomplish the same goals). All of the preceding characteristics listed in the previous chapters will help you have a servant's heart. I am amazed when I think about God's Son being a servant to others. He did not let

His power or authority remove the fact that He was a servant to their needs. Read what Pascarella said:

> For Christians and many others, Christ stands out in history as the ultimate servant. Paul instructs us to take that same servant stance. Your attitude should be the same as that of Christ Jesus. "Who being in very nature God, did not consider equality with God something to be grasped, but made himself nothing, taking the very nature of a servant, being made in human likeness. And being found in appearance as man, he humbled himself and became obedient to death-even death on the cross" (Philippians 2:6-8 NIV).[39]

Mercy is shown to others because a mercy leader is serving the needs of others. A servant's actions show mercy. For example, I fail in my life. I am not always the husband, father, son, friend, employee, and leader I should be. If I constantly focused on my failures, how could I even make it through this journey of life? However, when I experience mercy from my wife, children, family, friends, employer, and employees on some personal level, I feel they have shown mercy because they care about me and love me. We all need to feel valued and loved. As mercy leaders, we are fulfilling that need for our employees. Because we have humbled ourselves to become servants, we choose to put others before our own needs. We choose to show mercy to those who may fail us, and by exemplifying that mercy, we serve their human need.

Margaret Thatcher, former prime minister of England, once stated, "Being in power is like being a lady. If you have to remind people that you are, you aren't."[40] What does this statement mean? Reminding people who the leader is means there is no respect for the leader. I have been told in my leadership journey that people respect me as a leader. Although I appreciate those comments, it is sometimes difficult for me to realize I'm in a senior leadership position or see myself as a leader. I sometimes still have that small-town boy feeling.

I haven't disclosed this to many people but in high school I was bullied along with others. There was a guy in my high school who punched people on purpose during lunch time. It happened routinely and it was a miserable time for me because I was one of his victims. Apparently, he had a control issue and wanted to let people know that he was the "man". I knew that if I did anything back to him, I would pay with more physical abuse. I retreated to another location and tried to avoid him as much as possible. I eventually moved to another school because of a family move, and this provided some degree of relief. I learned early in my life that power and control was not what I wanted to part of. Although this situation was difficult, it brought some assistance in shaping me into who I am today because instead of seeking to influence through power and control, I want to influence through serving. I have learned to get rid of the "not good enough" mentality and embrace my role to use it to help others. Looking back on this statement as well as Margaret Thatcher's statement, I believe people respect me in my role because I am willing to use it to help them and the organization. I want to serve both my employees and my organization.

So how do we become a servant to others? It has to start with the leader who feels that he/she wants to serve. R. K. Greenleaf said, "Then conscious choice brings one to aspire to lead. The best test is: do those served grow as persons; do they, while being served, become healthier, wiser, freer, more autonomous, more likely themselves to become servants?"[41] A servant's heart allows a leader to use persuasion instead of authority in getting others to achieve his vision. They seek "to convince others, rather than coerce compliance. The servant leader is effective at building consensus within groups."[42]

Greenleaf writes, "Servant leadership works like the consensus building that the Japanese are famous for. Yes, it takes a while on the front end; everyone's view is solicited, though everyone also understands that his view may not ultimately prevail. But once the consensus is forged, watch out: With everybody on board, your so-called implementation proceeds wham-bam."[43] I'm not implying you will receive wham-bam results, but I do believe you will find that if your intent is to serve the needs of others, you will receive a servant mentality back from your employees. You will help create an environment that allows people to express their needs. As you and the organization attempt to meet those needs, productivity and the retention percentage of employees will increase. One again, there is a trend of reciprocity found when including each characteristic.

Those who serve attempt to understand the best way to meet the needs of others. Sometimes this is brought through experience. I remember riding on my 10 speed bicycle down the side streets of Big Stone Gap, Virginia to go on a rescue squad call. As a young man eager to help and serve when the emergency call went out, I had purpose. Today, I am still eager to help and serve because it gives me the same feeling. As a mercy leader, part of the purpose is serving others and sometimes as leaders we may lose sight of this. The weight of the role may dampen our initial calling. However, I hope to encourage you to reignite your purpose. Leadership is more than just having the power to have someone do what you say or the ability to earn a big salary. It is the ability to serve and help others.

Serving others may not come naturally to some people, especially if they have conflicts with another person. This may be a component of leadership that has to be developed. The key is to have the desire to change yourself and develop this component. Kuczmarski made the following observation:

> No one learns how to play the piano just by sitting back and looking at it. Nor does one learn how to play baseball by watching—the skills of catching, batting, and throwing can't be acquired through observation. Rather, the pianist and baseball player have to practice their respective skills over and over again, until playing a song or hitting a ball has been accomplished. There is always room for continued improvement, too. Most skills, regardless of the "sport," are learned by doing. This is true with leadership skills as well.[44] We must be willing to continue developing our leadership skills and as you do so, you will find it becomes easier.

I've heard a story about a leader whose purpose was to communicate to people about who His father really was. His father was well known throughout the world but seemed to be misunderstood. People feared Him, and from the stories they had heard about past history, they did not truly understand that the leader's father exhibited all the previous characteristics listed in this book. As the leader went through different regions talking about His father, He also became popular. His popularity attracted both positive and negative reactions. Although He attracted negative attention, He continued to hold steadfast to His convictions and serve other people. This leader did not let others sway what He believed, because He knew His purpose.

Do you know your purpose? If you are a leader or are contemplating entering into a leadership role, one of your purposes is to serve the needs of those you lead. In my example, the leader is Jesus. He came to this earth to communicate to others about God, His father. Jesus talked about loving others and showing forgiveness and exemplified humility, understanding, and care for others. He also knew a time would come when He would have to sacrifice His life for the needs of others. Jesus did serve the needs of others by sacrificing His life on a cross so we could receive salvation.

You may question how this example relates to you. The answer is simple. You must also be willing to serve the needs of others. Your leadership role may attract both positive and negative reactions, but you must stand firm with your beliefs and continue with your purpose. The act of dying on the cross for others also opened a way for us to be able to know God's mercy. Jesus' intent to serve our needs allowed us to experience mercy. This is very important to consider because, as already noted, servanthood is a component of a merciful leader. Your act of serving others will enable you to allow others to experience mercy.

We do not serve others expecting them to give back with a sense of self-interest. "The servant leader must empower followers instead of using power to dominate them."[45] Mercy leaders seek to better the lives of others. This should be their cause. Consider the following examples:

1. With a cause, Samson won many battles. Without one, he couldn't beat the temptation posed by Delilah.
2. With a cause, Saul conquered the kingdom. Without one, he could not conquer even his own jealousy.
3. With a cause, David conquered Goliath. Without one, he could not conquer his own lust.
4. With a cause, Elijah prayed down fire from heaven and beat 450 prophets of Baal. Without one, he ran in fear from a solitary woman—Jezebel.
5. With a cause, Simon Peter preached at Pentecost, and 3,000 people were saved. Without one, he denied he even belonged to the crowd that followed Jesus.[46]

Servanthood may sometimes receive negative attention, but it leads us to our next characteristic—courage.

TIME FOR REFLECTION—SERVICE

1. If you promote a culture that focuses on service to customers, do you also serve the needs of your employees?
2. Do you realize what your purpose is as a leader?
3. Do you serve others expecting to receive something back from them?

Service is an essential characteristic of a mercy leader. As noted in this chapter, when showing mercy to someone, you are actually serving their needs. Do not serve others because you want them to serve you. Practice this characteristic because you value them as an employee. This will have a reciprocal effect, because the employees will sense your sincerity.

CHAPTER 8
MERCIFUL LEADERS SHOW COURAGE

"With courage you will dare to take risks, have the strength to be compassionate and the wisdom to be humble. Courage is the foundation of integrity." [47]

—Keshavan Nair

At times as a merciful leader, you might find that showing mercy is unpopular. At times as leaders, we make decisions or complete actions that raise questions from others. Sometimes these questions and actions are unpopular. As leaders, though, we are in positions that create influence. It's how we create the influence that has such a profound impact on others. Creating influence through merciful leadership requires courage. Although we can all remember examples in our careers that required courage, I remember a specific situation when I became an interim director of a department. One of the employees in that department was not performing his duties. The morale of the department had decreased, and I was concerned about this situation. Certain disciplinary actions were supposed to be taken, but they had not happened. The proper orientation had also not been completed. My first instinct was to show mercy and give the employee every opportunity to show improvement, but staff members did not seem to understand my decision. They were frustrated with this employee and the lack of performance. Because of that, they were being forced to perform other duties in addition to their own.

My decision was unpopular, but I wanted to ensure that we were being fair to the employee. I was the controller of the situation and had to stand by my decision. It was important to me to do the right thing. It takes courage to continue with an unpopular decision. Like my case, you may sometimes be required to show mercy when others want you to judge. Merciful leadership takes courage, just like anything else worth doing.

According to Cavasin, "Courage in leadership is often thought of as the willingness to take risks, but it goes much deeper than that; courage is personal. It is fundamentally about authenticity: Know yourself; understand and overcome your fears and anxieties; present only your true face to the world."[48] Knowing yourself and then becoming transparent takes courage. In my own example, my concern about the morale of the department could have caused me to rush disciplinary actions, but I believed the employee should have been given every opportunity to improve. My integrity and character would not allow me to change my decision. Can you think of situations in your career in which you have made unpopular decisions? Did you have the courage to continue with those decisions?

Some components of courage[49] include:

1. "Increased alignment with your true values, purpose, and higher potential." Your purpose as a mercy leader is to lead others by showing mercy. Values are also considered.

2. "Greater momentum toward a revitalized vision and renewed sense of the group's purpose." As a mercy leader who consistently shows mercy and exhibits all of the listed characteristics, you will encourage your employees to have a sense of belonging to the organization because they are valued. They will follow where you lead.

3. "Higher morale among employees." The employees will sense you have courage to make difficult decisions even when they are not popular. They will respect you because you show mercy and are fair.

4. "The infusion of new ideas and recalibrating of outdated or stifling process." The first chapter of this book addressed the former perception of leadership and how this style of leadership is not appropriate in this decade. Mercy leaders are exhibiting a new leadership paradigm that will prove to have a positive impact in organizations and in the lives of merciful leaders and/or employees.

5. "More authentic, dynamic, and effective communication." Merciful actions communicate to the employee that you as the leader, as well as the organization, value that person.

People may feel uncomfortable exhibiting courage because this may be perceived as having an increased potential for "rocking the status quo" and would demand they walk the talk about values, mission, and purpose.

Winston Churchill once said, "Courage is the first of human qualities because it is the quality which guarantees all others."[50] Why? With courage, we are determined to include our other qualities. With courage, we will show mercy which requires us to forgive, love, have compassion, understand, be humble, and serve others. Author Martha Lasley wrote that the word "courage" comes from the French word for heart, *coeur,* meaning the ability to stand by one's heart or to stand by one's core."[51] Just as our heart is an essential component of our body that moves blood throughout our entire body, we find that when focusing on leadership, courage is an essential component. As leaders, we must be bold and show who we truly are and not have any fear when being a mercy leader. Where would you be if you listened to people who have told you certain goals could not be accomplished? Perhaps you have made decisions people have questioned and thus discouraged you, but you stood by your intuition that the decision was right. You had the courage to face adversity.

As a mercy leader, your overall goal is to show mercy. It takes courage to be a mercy leader, and it also takes courage to determine how you will show mercy to others. Employees will show more respect for you when you have the courage to stand by your decisions despite what others may think. I have learned that when I make decisions, I am the one who has to uphold my character and integrity. If I did not value my character and integrity, I could change my decisions based on what was popular. However, I have reached a point in my life, that although I do value what others think about me, this cannot be the driving force of my decision making. We are not in high school anymore. It is time to take a stand. Have the courage to be a mercy leader!

Having courage leads us to our last characteristic. Courage, or determination, will allow us to be committed to being a merciful leader.

TIME FOR REFLECTION—COURAGE

1. Do you make decisions based on popularity?
2. Are you willing to show mercy even when your decision may seem unpopular?
3. Do you encourage others to have courage when making decisions?

Courage is a critical component of being a mercy leader. Have you ever met leaders who make decisions based on their popularity? They tickle the ears of people by telling them what they want to hear, because the leaders want to be liked. I want to be a leader who has the courage to take a stand for what is right, not for what is popular. Merciful leadership may not always seem popular, but this leadership paradigm considers the employees, not popularity.

CHAPTER 9
MERCIFUL LEADERS ARE COMMITTED

"Commitment is the enemy of resistance, for it is the serious promise to press on, to get up, no matter how many times you are knocked down."[51]

—David McNally

Merciful leaders are committed! Of all the characteristics provided in this book, I wanted to include this as the last one because it shows a form of consistency and is all-inclusive. The *Merriam-Webster Online Dictionary* defines being committed as obligating or pledging oneself.[53] A mercy leader pledges or commits to show mercy in all situations. This commitment requires a consistency in all characteristics.

1. If you commit to be a mercy leader, you commit to forgive others. A mercy leader does not commit to forgive some employees while judging others. Forgiveness should be shown to all employees in the appropriate situations.

2. If you commit to be a mercy leader, you commit to love others. This love is consistent and an unconditional love.

3. If you commit to be a mercy leader, you commit to show compassion to your employees. We don't superficially say

we care about others. We prove our compassion by our actions.

4. If you commit to be a mercy leader, you commit to understand your employees. This might seem unobtainable at first, but as you seek to understand your employees, you will begin to understand who they are and their issues. This understanding will lead to wisdom.

5. If you commit to be a mercy leader, you commit to humble yourself. It is not about you but about the organization and those you lead. Be mindful of your intentions when showing mercy to others. People will know your sincerity or lack thereof and will base their trust on your intent.

6. If you commit to be a mercy leader, you commit to serve those you lead. The action of mercy ultimately serves the needs of others. Employees are searching for a leader who values them and is willing to serve their needs by not being judgmental. They need a leader who will show them mercy, and through this mercy, that leader is investing time to develop the employee.

7. If you commit to be a mercy leader, you commit to have courage to show mercy. Despite the opinion of others, your commitment and courage will be the gateway to actions of mercy.

8. If you commit to be a mercy leader, your commitment is a pledge to remain consistent in your actions.

To each person, commitment may mean something different. John Maxwell offers a few examples of what commitment is.

1. To the boxer, it's getting off the mat one time more than you've been knocked down.

2. To the marathoner, it's running another ten miles when your strength is gone.

3. To the soldier, it's going over the hill, not knowing what's waiting on the other side.

4. To the missionary, it's saying good-bye to your own comfort to make life better for others.

5. To the leader, it's all that and more because everyone you lead is depending on you.[54]

The last statement is powerful. Do you realize that everyone you lead is depending on you? When I was a frontline staff member, I liked it when my leaders made rounds and took the time to talk to me. Just a simple comment made me feel good inside because the leader of the organization knew my name and seemed to value me as an employee. Something simple like this showed their commitment to us—a commitment on which we all relied. We depended on the leader to ensure the organization would operate successfully so we would have a place to be employed. Your staff members also depend on you. As a leader, you are expected to lead the organization through difficult times, but you are also expected to satisfy their needs. This dependence or expectation can sometimes seem like a huge weight on your shoulders. Merely focusing on your purpose and commitment to the staff and organization will lead you through the difficult times.

As leaders, we have been committed to many different things. We were committed at first to education and then to our careers. When I began my career in healthcare, I was committed to reaching the top. It was the perfect example of a selfish ambition and a selfish commitment. A person focused like this cannot commit to being a mercy leader. The opposite is true. What are you committed to in your own life? If we took the energy we expend in activities that benefit only us and used it in being committed to our employees and organizations, the impact would be enormous.

That kind of commitment drives leaders to improve. This commitment develops not only you but also others. Committed leaders stand up and lead when times are tough. They do not walk away from their organizations or employees. We've all heard the saying, "When the going gets tough, the tough get going."[55] I would like to add this: When the going gets tough, committed leaders continue to lead. Why? Because their interest and focus are on the employees and the organization.

I recall a time when my commitment was challenged. During a difficult time in one of my leadership roles, my supervisor, Megan Schmidt, asked me to come to her office. She told me she had concern about my commitment to my role. I was initially frustrated with the conversation because although I was in a leadership role, I had been working side by side with my employees for a few days in a row to ensure patients were provided quality care. The hospital had been experiencing significant staffing issues so I was assisting with patient care. She challenged me to think about my commitment and then have a follow up discussion. I felt more committed than ever because I had been helping my team. However, she noticed my non-verbal communication was telling a different story. When I had the follow-up discussion, my commitment in the leadership role had been re-ignited. It took Megan's commitment to my success to identify that I was struggling. Through her commitment, I was able to identify an opportunity to enhance my own.

We should have a willingness to be merciful to others even when they are being rebellious or even when others are having a struggle. I want to make a point again that sometimes employees have to be disciplined or even terminated, but our commitment leads us to mercy before judgment. We will find that mercy brings commitment from the employee before judgment can.

Although commitment is the last characteristic I have included in this book, a mercy leader has even more characteristics. These characteristics will naturally bloom as you take the time and energy to become a merciful leader. It isn't easy! It isn't the way we have all been taught, but it is important for you and your employees in the long run that you commit to this leadership journey. When you catch yourself going back to your old habits of snap judgments, please do not be discouraged. I know your time is valuable and consumed with day-to-day cares. You may feel you do not have the energy to take the time to be merciful. In the long run, you will have a healthier organization, more productive employees who have been fully developed, and less stress in your own position.

TIME FOR REFLECTION—COMMITMENT

1. Are you committed to be merciful to others in your organization?
2. Are you committed to give yourself fully to your organization and employees?
3. Are you committed to being a mercy leader?

As you have read this book, I hope you have committed to being a mercy leader. This requires a consistency in showing mercy to all employees. As noted, mercy sometimes will also require discipline, but your willingness to treat all employees equally will gain tremendous respect from them. Be committed to your leadership role, and as you develop into a mercy leader, you will also experience mercy.

FROM THE HEART OF A MERCY LEADER

I want to speak to you from my heart. When God first gave me the idea of merciful leadership, I was early in my leadership career. Through bad decisions and less than perfect interactions with others, I have gained a lot of knowledge and experience. In my first book, I envisioned what I wanted to be and how I viewed other leaders. Now I have updated this work to include who I am, what I continue to want to be, and still how I view others. I am a **Mercy Leader**! The executive title does not matter. What matters more to me is being known as a mercy leader. What matters to me is how I can use mercy to transform the lives of others. There are times that I battle myself and question my own abilities as a leader. There are times that I do not believe in myself and wonder how I have been successful in my career. It is seemingly unexplainable. The explanation that I can give is the formula that has been given in this book. During my career, I have shown people they are valued. My executive positions have allowed me the opportunity to show each characteristic of a mercy leader. God has placed opportunities and people in my life who share the same values, and through this, success has followed.

In this paradigm of merciful leadership, you will find yourself continually giving to others. You will forgive, love, have compassion, care, attempt to understand others, humble yourself for others, serve others, have courage, and be committed to others. The constant giving may lead to exhaustion. I want to encourage you that it's worth it.

I recall something that happened in my career. A CEO came to me and stated that her Chief Nursing Officer had asked how I was doing. When she mentioned the CNO's name, I did not remember meeting her. However, while she was at another hospital that I visited during my regional executive role, I had made a lasting impression. This impression was so significant, she still remembered me years later. I was astounded and reminded of the importance of how we act in our roles.

As a mercy leader, the actions you take will make an impression on others. You can change the course of someone's career and life. There are times the happenings of the day may change your attitude, energy level, and willingness to be a mercy leader. However, I want to challenge you to be a day changer. Go change your day by showing forgiveness, love, and compassion. Seek to understand and be humble while serving others. Be courageous and committed in your leadership journey to be a mercy leader.

My daughter read my first book and being 18 years old at the time, she provided a summary of the entire book into one statement. After reading her statement and then reflecting on what it meant, I want to provide to you the following summation which I carefully put at the end so you wouldn't see it until now-

Mercy Leader-

Forgiving Love that requires **Compassion** and **Understanding** of followers from a **Courageous** and **Committed** leader.

Go Be a Mercy Leader!

ENDNOTES

[1] Obtained from
http://www.xmission.com/~westra/judgquot.htm.

[2] Filson, B. "CEOs and Boards Are Locked in a Spiral of Doom."
The Filson Leadership Group Inc., 2005. Available at
http://www.actionleadership.com/articles/0024.html.

[3] Winston, B. "Be a Leader for God's Sake." *School of Leadership
Studies* (Virginia Beach, VA: Regent University, 2002), 70.

[4] Jones, L.B. *Jesus, CEO: Using Ancient Wisdom for Visionary
Leadership* (New York: Hyperion, 1995), 203.

[5] Hackman, M.Z. and C.E. Johnson, *Leadership--A Communication
Perspective,* 4th ed. (Long Grove, IL: Waveland Press Inc., 2004),
95.

[6] Jones, 204-205.

[7] Bell, C.R. *Managers as Mentors: Building Partnerships for Learning.*
2nd ed. (San Francisco: Berrett-Koehler Publishers, Inc., 2002),
63.

[8] Obtained from http://www.wisdomquotes.com/cat_love.html.

[9] Jones, 255-256.

[10] Winston, 5.

[11] *Ibid.*

[12] Myra, H. and M. Shelley, "Leading With Love — The Secret to Billy Graham's Remarkable Ministry to the World" (September/October 2005). Obtained from http://www.christianitytoday.com/tc/2005/005/2.40.html.

[13] *Ibid*.

[14] Hunter, J.C. *The World's Most Powerful Leadership Principle* (New York: Crown Business, 2004), 89.

[15] Hunter, 119.

[16] Obtained from http://www.prosperityparadigm.com/quotes/compassion.html .

[17] P. Pascarella, *Christ-Centered Leadership: Thriving in Business by Putting God in Charge* (USA: Prima Publishing, 1999), 161.

[18] B. Winston, *Be a Leader for God's Sake* (Virginia Beach, VA: School of Leadership Studies — Regent University, 2002), 70.

[19] A. Galy and J.M. Lelen, *The Friend of Sinners* (USA: Benziger Brothers, 1930), 1.

[20] C. Zust, "The Compassionate Leader." Obtained from http://www.emergingleader.com/article19.html.

[21] *Ibid*.

[22] Obtained from http://www.heartquotes.net/Leadership.html.

[23] Daft, R.L. *Organization Theory and Design*, 8th ed. (Mason, OH: South-Western, 2004), 380.

24 Obtained from http://changingminds.org/disciplines/leadership/followership/follower_liking.htm.

25 Spears, L.C. *Robert Greenleaf—Servant Leadership* (Mahwah, NJ: Paulist Press, 2002), 313.

26 Hunter, 114.

27 Phillips, D.T. *Lincoln on Leadership—Executive Strategies for Tough Times* (New York: Warner Books, Inc., 1992), 13.

28 *Ibid*.

29 Ibid., 16.

30 Obtained from http://www.wisdomquotes.com/cat_humility.html.

31 Wofford, J.C. *Transforming Christian Leadership: 10 Exemplary Church Leaders* (Grand Rapids: Baker Books, 1999), 174.

32 Richards, N. *Humility* (Philadelphia: Temple University Press, 1992), 187.

33 Maxwell, J.C. *The Maxwell Leadership Bible* (Nashville: Thomas Nelson Publishers, 2002), 50.

34 *Ibid*.

35 Winston, 22.

36 Richards, 187.

37 Obtained from http://www.wisdomquotes.com/cat_leadership.html.

38 Obtained from http://www.greenleaf.org/leadership/servant-leadership/Robert-K-Greenleaf-Bio.html.

39 Pascarella, 131.

40 Hunter, J.C. *The Servant—A Simple Story About Leadership* (USA: Prima Publishing, 1998), 15.

41 Greenleaf, R.K. *The Servant Leader Within—A Transformative Path* (Mahwah, NJ: Paulist Press, 2003), 13.

42 "10 Principles of Servant Leadership." Obtained from http://www.butler.edu/studentlife/hampton/principles.htm.

43 Greenleaf, 25.

44 Kuczmarski, S.S. and T.D. Kuczmarski, *Values-Based Leadership: Rebuilding Employee Commitment, Performance and Productivity* (Paramus, NJ: Prentice-Hall, 1995), 202.

45 Yukl, G. *Leadership in Organizations,* 5th ed. (Upper Saddle River, NJ: Prentice Hall, 2002), 404.

46 Maxwell, J.C. *The Maxwell Leadership Bible.* (Nashville: Thomas Nelson, 2002), 1,097.

47 Obtained from http://www.wisdomquotes.com/cat_courage.html.

48 Cavasin, V. "On Becoming a Great Leader"(2007). Obtained from http://www.detroitchamber.com/detroiter/articles.asp?cid=103&detcid= .

49 *The Elements of Courageous Leadership.* Obtained from http://www.ivysea.com/pages/ldrex_0302_02.html.

[50] Homoly, P.A. "Leadership Takes Courage," *The Journal of Cosmetic Dentistry* (Volume 20, Issue 3, Fall 2004). Obtained from http://articles.paulhomoly.com/Leadership-Takes-Courage.pdf.

[51] Lasley, M. "Courage Is the Foundation of Leadership" (1999). Obtained from http://www.leadershipthatworks.com/Articles/Courage.htm.

[52] Obtained from http://www.leadershipnow.com/commitmentquotes.html.

[53] Obtained from http://www.m-w.com/dictionary/Committed.

[54] Vannoy, S. and C. Ross, "The Power of a Punch" (2005). Obtained from http://www.pathwaystoleadership.com/sv-colm09-05.html.

[55] Obtained from http://quotations.about.com/b/2005/07/06/when-the-going-gets-tough-the-tough-get-going.htm.

WORKS CITED

Bell, C.R. *Managers as Mentors: Building Partnerships for Learning.* 2nd ed. San Francisco: Berrett-Koehler Publishers, Inc., 2002.

Cavasin, V. "On Becoming a Great Leader" (2007). Obtained from http://www.detroitchamber.com/detroiter/articles.asp?cid=103 &detcid= .

Daft, R.L. *Organization Theory and Design.* 8th ed. Mason, OH: South-Western, 2004.

Filson, B. "CEOs and Boards Are Locked in a Spiral of Doom." The Filson Leadership Group Inc., 2005. Available at http://www.actionleadership.com/articles/0024.html.

Galy, A., and J.M. Lelen. *The Friend of Sinners.* USA: Benziger Brothers, 1930.

Greenleaf, R.K. *The Servant Leader Within—A Transformative Path.* Mahwah, NJ: Paulist Press, 2003.

Hackman, M.Z. and C.E. Johnson. *Leadership—A Communication Perspective,* 4th ed. Long Grove, IL: Waveland Press Inc., 2004.

Homoly, P.A. "Leadership Takes Courage." *The Journal of Cosmetic Dentistry* (Volume 20, Issue 3, Fall 2004). Obtained from http://articles.paulhomoly.com/Leadership-Takes-Courage.pdf.

Hunter, J.C. *The Servant—A Simple Story About Leadership.* USA: Prima Publishing, 1998.

Hunter, J.C. *The World's Most Powerful Leadership Principle.* New York: Crown Business, 2004.

Jones, L.B. *Jesus, CEO: Using Ancient Wisdom for Visionary Leadership.* New York: Hyperion, 1995.

Kuczmarski, S.S. and T.D. Kuczmarski. *Values-Based Leadership: Rebuilding Employee Commitment, Performance, and Productivity.* Paramus, NJ: Prentice Hall, 1995.

Lasley, M. "Courage Is the Foundation of Leadership" (1999). Obtained from http://www.leadershipthatworks.com/Articles/Courage.htm.

Macquarrie, J. *The Humility of God.* Philadelphia: The Westminster Press, 1978.

Maxwell, J.C. *The Maxwell Leadership Bible.* Nashville: Thomas Nelson Publishers, 2002.

Myra, H. and M. Shelley. "Leading With Love—The Secret to Billy Graham's Remarkable Ministry to the World" (2005). Obtained from http://www.christianitytoday.com/tc/2005/005/2.40.html.

Pascarella, P. *Christ-Centered Leadership: Thriving in Business by Putting God in Charge.* USA: Prima Publishing, 1999.

Phillips, D.T. *Lincoln on Leadership—Executive Strategies for Tough Times.* New York: Warner Books Inc., 1992.

"Principles of Servant Leadership." Obtained from http://www.butler.edu/studentlife/hampton/principles.htm.

Richards, N. *Humility.* Philadelphia: Temple University Press, 1992.

Spears, L.C. *Robert Greenleaf—Servant Leadership.* Mahwah, NJ: Paulist Press, 2002.

"Ten Principles of Servant Leadership." Obtained from http://www.butler.edu/studentlife/hampton/principles.htm.

"The Elements of Courageous Leadership." Obtained from http://www.ivysea.com/pages/ldrex_0302_02.html.

Vannoy, S. and C. Ross. "The Power of a Punch" (2005). Obtained from http://www.pathwaystoleadership.com/sv-colm09-05.html.

Winston, B. "Be a Leader for God's Sake." *School of Leadership Studies*, Virginia Beach, VA: Regent University, 2002.

Wofford, J.C. *Transforming Christian Leadership: 10 Exemplary Church Leaders.* Grand Rapids: Baker Books, 1999.

Yukl, G. *Leadership in Organizations.* 5th ed. Upper Saddle River, NJ: Prentice Hall, 2002.

Zust, C. "The Compassionate Leader." Obtained from http://www.emergingleader.com/article19.shtml.

INTERNET SOURCES CITED

http://changingminds.org/disciplines/leadership/followership/foll ower_liking.htm.

http://quotations.about.com/b/2005/07/06/when-the-going-gets-tough-the-tough-get-going.htm.

http://www.heartquotes.net/Leadership.html.

http://www.leadershipnow.com/commitmentquotes.html.

http://www.m-w.com/dictionary/Committed.

http://www.prosperityparadigm.com/Quotes/Compassion.htm.

http://www.wisdomquotes.com/cat_courage.html.

http://www.wisdomquotes.com/cat_humility.html.

http://www.wisdomquotes.com/cat_leadership.html.

http://www.wisdomquotes.com/cat_love.html.

http://www.xmission.com/~westra/judgquot.htm.

www.ingramcontent.com/pod-product-compliance
Lightning Source LLC
Chambersburg PA
CBHW021504210526
45463CB00002B/876